Travail to Prevail

A key to "Experiencing the Heart of God"

Dr. Joseph Mattera

Independent self-publishing platform
Createspace

Copyright © 2014

www.createspace.com

Taken from *Praying Hyde*, edited by Captain
E.G. Carre, and published by Bridge-Logos,
Inc.

Taken from *The Autobiography of Charles G.
Finney* by Charles G. Finney. Bethany House
Publishers, a division of Baker Publishing
Group," Copyright © 2006, and "Used by
permission."

ISBN 9781499724219

Dedication:

I dedicate this book to all those faithful intercessors who are praying into the kingdom the destiny of families and nations.

I am also indebted to the historic writings that aided the formulation of my prayer contained in this book.

I want to thank my dear friend Dr Larry Keefauver for blessing me by editing the manuscript of this book.

Lastly, I want to thank my assistant Geraldine Sofia for doing an amazing job facilitating this project.

TABLE OF CONTENTS

PREFACE

Even though this short book was written by me in the late 1990's, God has never laid it upon my heart to release this work until now. I believe He wanted me to first release my four books on the Kingdom of God. Also, I had to modify the end since it was written before the terrorist attacks of September 11, 2001; but the amazing thing is, when rereading this book, I remembered the intense burden many of us had in the spirit starting in 1998 because we all sensed something awful was going to happen very shortly. I hope the following pages are not only a blessing, but an inspiration to go after God and pursue Him like never before.

(Joseph Mattera, November 27, 2013)

Sometime in 1999, the Lord laid on my heart the need for a book on the topic of "Travail". Though this is by far the most intense form of intercession described in the scriptures, very little has been written about it, and to my knowledge there are no prominent books on the subject available. When I mentioned to a leading Christian author my plans for writing on this subject his response was, "How can you write a whole book on it?" This is precisely why I believe there is a great need in this area.

Due to my desire to make this book relevant, and to my lack of ability to find many other referents, I have had to write about my own personal experiences. I am very hesitant about this for a number of reasons.

1. I don't feel comfortable talking about my personal prayer life.

2. I don't feel comfortable talking about my experiences of personal intimacy with the Lord (sort of like taking a third party with you on your honeymoon or romantic vacation).

3. The tendency of some is to think of people with spiritual experiences "higher than they ought to."

Nevertheless, in spite of my hesitation, I believe those reading this book will be more enhanced and receive a greater impartation because of its personal touch. My greatest desire for this book is that it would inspire many to go beyond just "saying prayers" but to seek God's face, and to give those experiencing deep seasons of prayer encouragement and a biblical basis to keep growing in God.

CHAPTER 1
INTRODUCTION

It was a Monday night in early January 1999. I had received a word a few weeks before that Jesus was going to walk through our city and do "inventory". By inventory I mean that Jesus would examine the church and people of the city before He decides whether to visit our city with judgment or revival, or a combination of both. (In Genesis 18:20-22, Jehovah personally examined Sodom and Gomorrah before He judged it.) In response to this, our church had a solemn assembly in which we met every night for five days, interceding for our city.

On the first night of our solemn assembly, I was running about fifteen minutes late. As I was driving to the church I expected to find only a handful of people, unfocused and scattered in their prayers. Upon entering the sanctuary, I was shocked at what I found! Almost half of the sanctuary was filled with the most intense corporate prayer I had ever heard. Men and women groaning bent over as if in great pain, grownups and children laying prostrate and even eerie shrieks coming from all over the room. I had seen individuals in this kind of intense prayer, but never had I ever seen a church prayer meeting where the whole atmosphere was charged with such an intense identification with and urgency for the will of God to be done. Usually prayer meetings can work up to something like this but this was only the first fifteen minutes of the meeting. I knew we were onto something big. Something that could change the destiny of a city!

Chapter 2

My Story

When I came to Christ in January of 1978, I was the kind of person that could read the bible for many hours, but I had a hard [difficult] time praying for more than a couple of minutes.

All that changed in June of 1978 when I received the baptism of the Holy Spirit and began to speak in tongues. Within a few months I was able to pray for a long time without getting bored.

Occasionally, while I was praying for something, my heart started getting weighed down with the burden of the thing I was praying for. It was so heavy with the sense of why I was praying that I had a difficult time having a conversation with someone. I could barely do anything else but pray because my mind and heart was so preoccupied with this intense weight or burden. When this "spirit of prayer" came on me, the kind when my whole being was engulfed in prayer, I would try to alter my schedule and steal away from all regular work and the company of others. I would get alone and pray until the burden of the thing I was praying for would lift off of me and my heart would be filled with the peace and assurance of God. Through the years this spirit of prayer would only come upon me occasionally. Then it would come upon me for days at a time – then weeks – most of the time I couldn't even use my known language (English) and after some years, the intensity of the burden even transcended "speaking in tongues" with most of my time spent groaning in the presence of God, knowing that I was standing in the gap for something.

(Before I go on, I want the reader to realize something important. You can pray anytime you want but you can't make [cause] "the spirit of prayer" to come upon you. You can't just decide that you want to go into "travail". It comes upon you only when God wills it to happen, usually when you begin to intercede for something and you strike a "nerve" in the spirit. God enlarges your heart and you begin to pray supernaturally with an intensity that can only come from God).

It got to the point in the late 80's that I realized about 95% of the time when I began to pray I would tap into God's heart for the thing I was praying for and then I would go into travail with varying degrees of time spent praying fervently according to the need.

I remember a time in the early 1990's when I went to a conference hosted by an apostolic network. A pastor I had only met a few times before was driving me there.

We had a five-hour drive ahead of us and he asked me to pray traveling mercies for us before we started out. Well, I not only prayed for traveling mercies, but an incredible burden for the conference and the network came upon me and I went into intense travail for the entire five-hour trip. (I couldn't help but wonder what this pastor thought of me when I not only prayed in tongues but began moaning and groaning because of the intense weight of the purposes of God on my soul. I figured God knew what He was doing when He put it upon me and I threw "caution to the wind" and then, you know what; the spirit of travail came upon him as well.)

When I arrived at the conference the burden of God for the week-long conference was so great that I prayed about twelve hours a day mostly with groanings too deep for words (Romans 8:26,27). My heart was so heavy that I couldn't go to a single session or workshop. I had to force myself to go to the evening plenary sessions. I literally felt what God felt about the ministers, the conference and what God wanted to do for eternal fruit (at one point the travail of my soul was so great that I had to get people to take turns watching in prayer with me to help me bear the burden).

God showed me, after two days of intense prayer and travail, that the Wednesday and Thursday evening plenary sessions would be the most powerful the network had ever seen, catapulting ministers into the purposes of God way into the rest of the decade. Sure enough, the Wednesday night meeting was so powerful it ended at midnight. The Thursday night meeting ended almost at 1:00a.m. Friday morning, there was a powerful demonstration of praise, worship, prophecy and consecration to the mission field. All of these hours agonizing in prayer were worth it when I saw the marvelous way the Lord poured out His spirit and visited those ministers.

I have been living with this kind of prayer lifestyle for years, not knowing it could ever accelerate, but then came January 2, 1997.

As I said earlier, this spirit of prayer first came on me occasionally, then more frequently.

(Most of the time it came after I initiated prayer and intercession.) But on January 2, 1997, the spirit of prayer came upon me so mightily; it didn't even wait for me to begin to pray. I didn't even know why it accelerated on that particular date.

I must confess, many times to prevent the spirit of travail from coming on me, (so I could lead a somewhat normal life), I would purposely not even pray, consequently not giving it a chance to come upon me. That particular day I woke up with it upon me. This went on day after day, week after week, month after month. In the back of my mind I was thinking, *I will pray it through and it will leave me.* I found that I had now entered into a lifestyle of travail, with a spirit of prayer upon me anywhere from three to eight hours every day. (This lasted almost exactly three years until the beginning of January 2000). I had to alter my busy schedule to accommodate all the time I needed in prayer so I could function and fulfill the destiny of God. Altering my schedule had been no easy task in light of the fact I have a family that includes five children, a growing church, and an apostolic ministry to my city and various parts of the nation and the world.

Instead of waiting for it to leave me, I have embraced it and now I wouldn't want to live any other way. (The past two years since around 2012, this spirit of prayer usually comes upon me in the middle of the night so that every morning I wake up with an intense burden of prayer upon me that I push through until the weight on my soul is lifted. It frequently comes upon me again by late afternoon and then before I go to bed.)

CHAPTER 3

THE COST OF LIVING IN TRAVAIL:

THE TIME COMMITMENT

1. HAVING TO ALLOW FOR A GOOD PART OF YOUR TIME TO BE GIVEN OVER TO GOD IN DESPERATE PRAYER AND SEEKING HIM

As a result of living in this "lifestyle of travail", I try not to book my week up with appointments in the morning, giving myself a good part of every morning to spend time alone, wrestling in travail for the purposes of God.

For those God is calling to walk in a lifestyle of "travail", there will be frequent seasons when you will have to alter your plans because the spirit of prayer is upon you so mightily you scarcely can do anything *but* pray! Often I have to retreat from the company of others until the intense burden of my heart is lifted through travail. (After a while you can become so experienced that you learn how to travail silently in your spirit while in the company of others without them knowing about it.)

2. LIVING FREQUENTLY WITH AN INTENSE BURDEN

You have to learn to pray with an intense burden upon your heart, sometimes so intense you feel in great agony as God lays upon you the burdens of others in the spirit. An agony so great, sometimes you almost feel like you are going to die until your travail gives birth to an assurance of victory and peace. There have been people I know who have stopped praying for people because they started getting an intense burden for them. They couldn't handle the uncomfortable sense of entering into Christ's suffering for the person (literally getting a small glimpse of how God really sees a person). They probably don't realize that they are not only in disobedience concerning their lack in prayer, but they are stopping the Holy Spirit from using them to bring the other person victory.

3. WALKING IN THE FEAR OF THE LORD

Living with this kind of prayer life brings you deeply into the character and heart of God. Consequently, you begin to not only love the things God loves, but you also hate the things God hates. The deepness [dimension] of spiritual intimacy you develop throughout all the time spent in deep travail causes you to walk more in God's heart and character. Consequently, your conscience becomes very sensitive to those things that grieve the Holy Spirit. You come to a place where your thought life begins to become a sanctuary where God can dwell. Fleeting thoughts I was able to entertain without conviction years ago now cause me great conviction of soul. The flippant attitude, course jesting and irreverent conversation that many saints participate in will not do. After you leave a prayer closet in which you spent hours interceding, groaning and travailing for the sins of God's people, you will not be quick to join in [engage in] with the same kind of behavior. I literally tremble with the fear of the Lord when I speak about others and I try to weigh every word I speak.

4. BEING MISUNDERSTOOD

The average Christian's idea of intercession is praying over a "laundry list" of people's prayer requests and then moving on. This is good but there is something deeper. I have to be guarded how I pray in public because if I allow myself to go into travail, most saints in the body of Christ would think I'm weird. (I guess they're right!) My course of action over the years has been to spend a good amount of time in prayer *before* certain prayer meetings so I can pray the full burden of God out of me long before the prayer meeting begins. Then I can go about my business praying "normally" like the other saints.

5. IDENTIFYING WITH THE SPIRITUAL CONDITION OF THOSE AROUND YOU

Whenever I go to a conference or church, I begin to pick up the spiritual condition of those around me or I pick up the purpose of God for that church, ministry or person. As a result, I begin to enter into travail for those involved and I need to spend extra time preparing before I minister or before I participate in that event. I can't just go preach, or be present and carry on with a "business as usual" mentality.

6. EXPERIENCING PHYSICAL DEMANDS

Sometimes hours of intense prayer can take a toll on you physically. Often, I am drenched with sweat after hours of intense travail. (Some people have actually thought I was involved in some kind of aerobic exercise. At times I wondered if I was breaking blood vessels in my face.)

The bible teaches us that after Jesus prayed in the garden of Gethsemane, an angel had to come down and strengthen Him and that He actually sweat drops of blood. His prayer was so intense he literally broke blood vessels.

David Breinerd, the great apostle to the Indians in the early 17th century, used to pray so intensely that all the snow around him in the forest where he was praying would melt. Due to the fact that prayer is so intense and the demand on the body so demanding, the Lord has instructed me to exercise regularly. Being in good physical condition is a plus if we are going to give ourselves over to God for a life of prayer.

7. CONCLUSION

There are other things I can give you to consider before you volunteer to embark on this intense "prayer journey". For now I will stop here, for

I think I have given you enough to ponder about

before you "sign up" to live a life of travail.

CHAPTER 4

THE PERSONAL BENEFITS OF TRAVAIL

I. YOU MEET THE NEED IN THE SPIRIT BEFORE YOU MEET IT IN THE FLESH

The way travail works is that God lays upon your heart the burden of how He feels about a person or situation. The weight of that burden pressing down on your heart compels you to go to God for relief. You confront the situation first in the spirit, before you (have to) deal with it in the flesh.

Often I have received a very strong spirit of prayer for one of my family members. As I'm in travail, I'll discern what it is for and then I'll keep praying and travailing until I push through to total victory and peace. Then, when, or if I'm confronted with the situation I was in travail for, it becomes another occasion for God's purposes to prevail and for victory. (Of course, there are some battles for my family members in the spirit that are ongoing and have caused me much travail through the years. Being in travail does not necessarily mean that all issues and challenges will just immediately disappear.)

One time, while I was away with my wife in Virginia, a mighty spirit of prayer came upon me. I was out on the beaches of Virginia for five hours, late at night, groaning and travailing in spirit. At first I didn't know what it was for, and then the Lord revealed to me that it was for one of my children back home in New York. I discerned that he was going to be confronted in a certain situation in school in two days and that he shouldn't give in to the temptation, that if he did, disaster could follow.

I then called him up and described the scenario in detail warning him not to fall into the trap. Though my son didn't come through the situation perfectly, (he did respond somewhat to the temptation), the altercation that followed was minimized and what could have been a major physical injury only turned out to be a minor one. I know that if I didn't meet this situation first in the spirit, my son wouldn't have had the proper prayer covering and he could have been killed in that incident.

Countless times I've been in travail for my family, church or ministry just before very difficult situations arose. Because I met the situation first in the spirit, took upon myself the full burden of it prophetically in prayer and travail, I was ready for it when I faced it in the natural. The result is I am able to walk in the purposes of God (though it seems as though I'm walking through mine fields) and remain emotionally unscathed in spite of the difficult circumstances I am faced with. (Sometimes this intense prayer enables you to go through difficult times, especially in cases when your answer to prayer in a difficult situation does not manifest itself immediately).

II. YOU ALLOW THE MIND AND CHARACTER OF CHRIST TO TRANSFORM YOUR THOUGHTS, FEELINGS AND ACTIONS

As already stated, when you are in travail, you become so intensely identified with those you are praying for, that God puts upon you their burdens and realities. You begin to feel the way God feels about the objects of your prayer and travail. Consequently, it enables a person to become more and more like God in their behavior and thought life. (Your heart and mind adjusting itself to the way God feels about people, places and things.)

III. YOU WALK IN DIVINE REVELATION

When you are in travail you are imbued with the mind and purposes of God for a person or situation. Consequently you begin to see things through God's eyes, not always the way others want you to see things. Travail develops your discernment for people, places and things, and it develops you in the prophetic giftings.

Every time I am in travail and push through in the spirit to victory I take a few minutes to discern what the Lord is saying. Many times I don't merely sense a word, but the intensity of my experience causes me to be filled with the knowledge of His will in all wisdom and spiritual understanding. (Colossians 1:9)

My whole being literally pulsates with the mind of God for a long time after I finish praying. For example I'll get a burden for a meeting, an event, or the city of New York or a place I am going to minister to. I pray for what the Lord put on my heart and I'll usually go into travail (a God-induced experience). After I pray through my whole being resonates with a word for that situation or person. Every citywide event I have initiated has come as a result of God speaking to me in this way. (I believe my travail gives birth to the event and then God fills me with a vision of what He just brought into existence along with a general strategy for how to carry it out.)

I remember recently being in a very high-level leadership meeting concerning a whole network of churches. I was in very heavy travail before the meeting and prayed through until my burden was lifted. As I was walking to the meeting I was innately aware that my whole being was filled with a word for those leaders (though I wasn't aware of praying for a word to speak to them, it just happens automatically after you finish the process of travail). I walked into that meeting and delivered the word with power and authority. Within minutes many of us were weeping, repenting and had a lot more clarity for our situation. Things like this happen all the time with travail. It gives you the mind of the Lord and the ability to deliver it with power and authority.

IV.   YOUR UNDERSTANDING OF THE WORD OF GOD INCREASES

After deep seasons of travail and waiting on God you are so in tune with the Holy Spirit that when you open up the bible the Holy Spirit will illuminate the scriptures as never before. That's not all! When you read, your spirit is able to assimilate truth and concepts as never before, and consequently you're able to remember much of what you've read (as opposed to just intellectually assimilating truth and acquiring mere head knowledge).

Many people think I spend much time studying because of all the writing and speaking I do, but the truth of the matter is, I usually pray much more then I study but my capacity to assimilate truth is amplified because of my lifestyle of prayer.

V.   YOU REACH A DEEPER SPIRITUAL INTIMACY WITH GOD

When you are in travail, your spirit is intensely interacting with the Holy Spirit. God literally searches the hearts of those in travail so we could pray according to the will of God.

> Romans 8:26, 27 reveals, "Likewise the Spirit also helpeth our infirmities: for we know not what we should pray for as we ought: but the Spirit itself maketh intercession for us with groanings which cannot be uttered. And he that searcheth the hearts knoweth what is the mind of the Spirit, because he maketh intercession for the saints according to the will of God."

All of the interaction between your spirit and God's Spirit in prayer builds you up in your faith and causes you to be strong spiritually. This not only changes your prayer life but also greatly enhances your walk with God.

VI. YOU MAINTAIN A STRONG COMMITMENT TO GOD, HIS CHURCH AND HIS KINGDOM

Anybody who allows themselves to enter into the sufferings of Christ in prayer and invests much of their time doing the same, will be highly committed, not only to God, but to His purposes, to His kingdom and to His Church. In travail, you literally feel what God feels about a person or situation. This binds you to what you are praying for in a way that can only be described as supernatural. It keeps you on your toes spiritually and keeps the fire of God burning in you continually. I believe with all my heart that the only way we can stay "on fire" for God is that we maintain a healthy, consistent, fervent time of seeking God's purposes and His face.

VII. TRAVAIL DEEPENS YOUR HUMILITY AND DEPENDENCY ON GOD

When you enter into travail, God unfolds unto you the ramifications of what you are praying for. You begin to understand the laws of sowing and reaping, the fear of God, destiny, and have a sober attitude about all of life. You begin to really appreciate every breath and take nothing you have for granted.

I believe most disasters in the church and world can be avoided if people only have the heart and mind of God. Rather than getting puffed up, travail brings you low, into an agony of soul, before you taste the fruit of victory.

> Matthew 5:4 – "Blessed are they that mourn: for they shall be comforted."
> Isaiah 53:11 – "He shall see of the travail of his soul, and shall be satisfied: by his knowledge shall my righteous servant justify many; for he shall bear their iniquities."

Big name ministers and celebrities never intimidate those who know God. Travail wipes away the awe and fear of man because we're all mere flesh and all we have that's good comes from God. (Though I respect all people and give honor to whom honor is due). I often say, "Once you've met with Him, everybody else is a disappointment."

CHAPTER 5

A BIBLICAL STUDY OF TRAVAIL

I strongly believe that we cannot base our beliefs merely on subjective experiences. There must be biblical principles, examples and precedent to substantiate it.

Philosophically, I can describe travail like this: if you can imagine the difference between experiencing a pain from pinching yourself with a needle and a horrible, throbbing toothache or earache. In the former, you can separate yourself from what you're feeling and objectively say you have a pain. (Your initial response to the pinch may be expressing yourself with a word like "ouch".)

In the latter, the pain is so great that it feels like your whole being is engulfed in it. You feel like you are in the pain; the pain actually becoming who you are. Your response to this pain is not merely "ouch" but constant groans and moans. Travail is like that. When you are merely praying a laundry list for somebody you feel somewhat concerned for them. When you are in travail, you are identified with them. Your whole being is weighted down with an agony for their physical or spiritual state.

Is there anything in the Bible that describes this? Absolutely. There are scriptural teachings, examples and principles that teach us about travail.

1.   SCRIPTURAL TEACHINGS

Romans 8:26 reads, "Likewise the Spirit also helpeth our infirmities: for we know not what we should pray for as we ought: but the Spirit itself maketh intercession for us with groanings which cannot be uttered."

I used to believe this verse was referring to "speaking in tongues." A closer look at this passage indicates Paul is not talking about a verbal language, but "groanings". This word in the Greek is *stenagmos*, which translates as, to groan, to sigh, prayers to God expressed inarticulately; the sighing person is in distress. Surely, this does not necessarily reflect a "prayer language like tongues" but a prayer expressed by gut-level moans and groans that describes accurately the desperate condition of a human heart. God must be pleased with this type of prayer because it states that when someone is in this kind of deep intercession, it is actually the Holy Spirit praying inside of them.

Furthermore, verse 27 tells us that God actually searches the heart of the person in travail to find out what the mind of the Holy Spirit is concerning the people being prayed for.

Romans 8:27 reads, "And he that searcheth the hearts knoweth what is the mind of the Spirit, because he maketh intercession for the saints according to the will of God."

2. SCRIPTURAL EXAMPLES

a) Jesus

In the Garden of Gethsemane, Jesus' condition when He began to pray describes travail perfectly.

Two common things experienced in travail is that you feel sorrowful (or an agony of soul) and a heaviness, burden or weight on your heart. Matthew 26:37 says that Jesus began to *be sorrowful* (*lupeomai*, to cause to grieve) and very heavy (*ademoneo*, overwhelmed with a burden; a synonym of *stenazo*, to groan). When you are in travail for someone, you are identified with them to the point in which you are weighted down in the spirit with a burden. This makes sense because in the garden of Gethsemane, Jesus was preparing Himself to go to the cross, where He would be bearing the sins and sicknesses of the entire world—the ultimate in identification.

> 1 Peter 2:24 – "Who his own self bare our sins in his own body on the tree, that we, being dead to sins, should live unto righteousness: by whose stripes ye were healed."
>
> Matthew 8:17 – "That it might be fulfilled which was spoken by Isaiah the prophet, saying, Himself took our infirmities, and bare our sicknesses."

2 Corinthians 5:21 – "For he hath made him to be sin for us, who knew no sin; that we might be made the righteousness of God in him."

b)   PAUL THE APOSTLE

Another example of somebody experiencing travail in the Bible is Paul. He so identified with the people he was ministering to, that it was reflected in the experiences of his heart. In describing how he felt about his fellow Jews, he says in Romans 9:2, that He had "great heaviness (lupe, i.e., grief, sorrow; synonym, *penthos*, a birth pang, travail) and continual sorrow" in his heart. I believe that in this verse he was referring back to what he taught in Romans 8:26.

In another instance, Paul was so burdened for the Galatian church because of their falling away, that he says in Galatians 4:19 that he had to "travail in birth again" for them "until Christ was formed in them".

Again he was referring to a time when intercession for the Galatian church got so intense that it changed from ordinary intercession to travail so that Christ could be formed in them. This shows us that travail is being pregnant with the needs of others; that we are to "push through" until we give birth to God's will for them.

c) Elijah the prophet

In 1 Kings 18:41-45 Elijah was praying bent down to the ground, with his face between his knees. Some people believe this is also an instance of "travailing" prayer.

3. SCRIPTURAL PRINCIPLES

This principle is also shown in Isaiah 66:8, "For as soon as Zion travailed, she brought forth her child." Generally, you can say common intercession is used by God to protect something that already exists and travail gives birth to something that didn't previously exist.

To eliminate confusion, let me summarize the different kinds of prayer taught in scripture. Ephesians 6:18 states, "pray always with all prayer"; can be translated "all kinds of prayer". Let us describe briefly some of these "kinds" of prayer found throughout Scriptures.

1.   Praise – a celebration of what God has done for us. This generally brings us into the gates of God, and can include exhortation of one saint to another.

> Psalm 100:4 – "Enter into his gates with thanksgiving, and into his courts with praise: be thankful unto him, and bless his name."

2.   Worship – more intimate than praise. Generally it refers to seeking God for who He is rather than merely thanking Him for what He has done. It is seeking God's face, not His hand. An example of this can be found when the elders, angels and living creatures surrounding God's throne in Revelation 4-5 who ascribe to the Lord His attributes and their adoration of Him.

3. Supplication – to camp out until God answers. To cry out to God continually for yourself or another until God answers.

4. Intercession – to make requests known unto God for a person.

5. Travail – an intense form of intercession in which you are pregnant with God's will for something and you push through (usually in the form of groaning) until you give birth in the spirit to victory.

CHAPTER 6

TRAVAIL CAN BE IMPARTED

For years I have always made it my top priority to spend much time seeking God's face and allowing God to birth things in me during prayer. The time I spend before the face of God is such a part of my life, both my wife, children and church staff have understood it and had to make allowances for it, especially during very deep and prolonged seasons of prayer and travail.

One day my wife received a word from the Lord that He wanted me to lay hands on my ministry team and impart my spirit of prayer and passion for Jesus into them. I thought it unusual, but after almost twenty years of marriage and serving with my wife in the ministry, I've learned to trust her prophetic words. (My wife is my greatest prophet and counselor; she is herself a great prayer warrior).

Over the years, I have preached on travail in various churches and occasionally in my own church, and during the altar ministry, I would lay hands on the respondents and most of them would receive a strong spirit of travail. Many of them would be bent over or lay on the floor in agony of soul for a long period of time. (I concluded that God moved this way only to confirm what I just preached. Not realizing I could impart this whether I preached on it or not.)

After my wife received that word, it opened up a whole new perspective on how God wanted to birth an intercessory prayer movement in our church and perhaps our city. I realized that, as leaders, we are responsible for a lot more than just teaching on prayer or praying with the saints. We are responsible to freely give what has been given to us by God (Matthew 10:8).

Consequently, as a response to my wife's prophetic word (in February of 1999), I determined to lay hands on my ministry team, our intercessors, and the congregants and impart to them my spirit of prayer and passion for Jesus. When I started doing it, the heavens burst open over our church. People were lying on the floor, or bent over in deep travail, weeping uncontrollably for our city. Children and teens fell on the floor writhing in agony for the sins of the church and the city. It not only released a spirit of travail toward objects of prayer, but people were released into having a passion for Jesus, seeking His face, not only His hand. (Or His works and deeds)

I remember well that morning service on the last Sunday in February 1999. I began to impart the spirit of travail and a passion for Jesus in our church. Within minutes, multitudes were on the floor, desperate for more of Jesus or writhing in agony for our city. Chairs were flying everywhere. It looked like a sea of the slain, total chaos, as people everywhere (not only at the altar) were moaning, groaning and in total desperation for Jesus and for revival. It's so contagious that many times someone would walk into an area where people are in travail and instead of leaving right away as they planned; they wind up staying for hours in travail themselves. The great thing is that those who don't receive this special "spirit of prayer" as just a one-time experience, but follow it up with a disciplined, consistent prayer life, have carried this impartation with them wherever they go.

One of the things we did in New York City in the late 1990s was to start a metro wide network of intercessors called "New York City Intercessors". Under the direction of Citynet founder, Nina Lemnah, under my oversight, pastors released to us hundreds of intercessors to gather monthly or bimonthly to pray for our city, for training and casting citywide vision. (No one was allowed to participate in NYC Intercessors without a pastor's recommendation and blessing.)

At these and other citywide meetings, I released many of the people from our congregation who have received this impartation (up to fifty people in our local church had this impartation at one time) and they have laid hands on intercessors from all over our city and the same thing occurs over and over again. Multitudes of people receive this spirit of prayer and passion for God and all over the sanctuary people are released into travail. It must have appeared like total pandemonium to some (the casual onlooker), however, to most of us it was the closest thing to heaven, we've ever seen.

In the past decades many believe God visited numerous churches with a renewal movement that were accompanied by laughter and the joy of the Lord and various manifestations of the Spirit. (Of course, not all of these manifestations were always authentic moves of God)

God is going to take the renewed Church to the logical next step. Not to laugh more, but to be identified with the sufferings of Christ, for His kingdom to come on earth, as it is in heaven. Renewal will never be enough to transform our cities. It's only meant to transform the Church so that we can then go forth and transform the world around us. Before we can have societal transformation, many things need to be in place. One of them is to have a remnant of people that will have an intense longing for God and for His purposes that are willing to lay down their agendas and push His purposes through in prayer until He gives us the victory. Attempting to transform a city or nation without the proper foundation of united prayer, intercession and travail will mean certain defeat.

We have to understand why God renews us to begin with. He brings us back to Him in renewal so that we can then identify with His purposes and stand in the gap for a lost and unredeemed society.

CHAPTER 7

HISTORICAL EXAMPLES

When these prolonged seasons of prayer began in my life in 1978, I had no frame of reference to validate my experiences except another young Christian who was my prayer partner and mentor. Unfortunately, I lost touch with him within a few years, but in the interim, he gave me some of his books. Two of these books were instrumental in helping me understand that what was happening was not something unique or new, but something God has used for centuries to birth His purposes. If it weren't for those books, many times I think I would have not only questioned my experiences, but my sanity.

In reading these books, I have found that the present day Church has lost much ground in the area of prayer. It is not enough just for pastors to come together and pray brief, perfunctory prayers. That will never bring transformation to a city. It is a good start but not enough. In the past moves of God, multitudes of people spent hours, days and months in intense, protracted travail before God would visit in revival and awakening. I will attempt, for now, to use several people as historical examples, but there are countless more that I could document.

<u>John Hyde</u>

John "Praying" Hyde was a missionary to India during the early 1900s. The forward to one biography of his life has these words:

> "We take our stand near the prayer closet of John Hyde, and one permitted to hear the sighing and the groaning and to see the tears coursing down his face, to see his frame weakened by foodless days and sleepless nights, shaken with sobs he pleads 'O God give me souls or I die."

Let's read the following powerful account:

> In one instance, as Hyde and others were in a prayer room during a convention, a young girl came and requested a prayer for her father.

(Her father had compelled her to neglect Christ's claims upon her.)

Hyde and the others "began to pray and suddenly the great burden of that soul was cast upon us and the room was filled with sobs and cries for one whom most of us had never seen or heard before. Strongmen lay on the ground groaning in agony for that soul. There was not a dry eye in that place until as last God gave us the assurance that prayer had been heard."

Reflecting on this story, one brother who was there wrote,

> "God wants those who are willing to bear the burden of the souls of these millions without God to go with Jesus unto Gethsemane. It is a blessed experience to feel that in some measure we can enter into the fellowship of Christ's sufferings. It brings us into a precious nearness to the Son of God. And not only this, but it is God's appointed way of bringing the lost sheep back into the fold."[1]

Page 84 recalls this story of Hyde:

---

[1] Praying Hyde, Captain E. C. Carre, pp. 23, 24

"One day the burden of prayer for the Europeans of the station had fallen on Hyde. For two or three days he never went to bed nor did he go down to meals and the food sent up to his room was generally carried down again untouched. How often he came and knelt by my bed that I might try to help him bear the burden. On Saturday night he was in great agony."

In another part of the book it tells of how the then world famous evangelist, Dr. Wilber Chapman, was having an unsuccessful evangelistic campaign. Until Hyde started praying, in Chapman's own words,

"At one of our missions in England, the audience was extremely small. Results seemed impossible, but I received a letter from a missionary that an American missionary known as "Praying Hyde" would be in the place to pray God's blessing down upon the work. Almost instantly, the tide changed—the hall was packed and my first invitation meant 50 men for Jesus Christ."[2] (Pages 108-109 of "Praying Hyde")

---

[2] Praying Hyde, Captain E. C. Carre, pp. 23, 24

Charles Finney and the Second Great Awakening

Charles Grandison Finney was perhaps America's greatest revivalist. He was instrumental in both the second and third Great Awakenings in our nation's history. Many of those converted in his meetings went on to become catalysts for social reform.

One of the most important things Finney did was write a book entitled, Revival Lectures. In this book Finney lays out the fundamental principles needed to start and maintain a revival. The following quotes are excerpts from this book. (Revival Lectures, Charles Finney, Revell)

> "Sometimes it happens that those who are the most engaged in employing truth (preaching) are not the most engaged in prayer.
> This is always unhappy, for unless they have the spirit of prayer (or unless someone else has) the truth, by itself, will do nothing but harden men in impenitence."(p. 50)
> "Prayer is not effectual unless it is offered up with an agony of desire. The apostle Paul

speaks of it as a travail of the soul. Jesus Christ, when He was praying in the garden, was in such agony that "His sweat were as it were great drops of blood falling to the ground: (Luke 22:44). I have never known a person sweat blood, but I have known a person pray till blood started from his nose. And I have known persons pray until they were all wet with perspiration in the coldest weather in winter. I have known persons pray for hours till their strength was all exhausted with the agony of their minds. Such prayers prevailed with God. (p. 58)

"Why God Requires Such Prayer (p. 65, 66)

Why does God require such prayer, such strong desires, and such agonizing supplications? These strong desires strongly illustrate the strength of God's feelings. They are like the real feelings of God for impenitent sinners."

"I have seen a man of as much strength of intellect and muscle as any man in the community fall down prostrate, absolutely overpowered by his unutterable desires for sinners. I know this is a stumbling block to many; and it always will be as long as there remain in the church so many blind and stupid professors of religion. But I cannot doubt that these things are the work of the spirit of God. Oh, that the whole church could be so filled with the spirit as to travail in prayer, till a nation should be born in a day! (Isaiah 66:8)

In talking about the spirit of prayer and travail, Finney says,

"Do you think that such things are new in the experience of believers? If I had time, I could show you, from President Edwards (evangelist Jonathan Edwards, a revivalist in the early 17th century) and other approved writers (had) cases and descriptions just like this."

(P.70)

"This travailing in birth for souls also creates a remarkable bond of union between warm hearted Christians and young converts. Those who are converted appear very dear to the hearts that have had this spirit of prayer for them. The feeling is like that of a mother for her firstborn. Paul expresses it beautifully in Galatians 4:19 – "My little children, of whom I travail in birth again until Christ be formed in you."

In a revival, I have often noticed how those who had the spirit of prayer loved the young converts. I know this is all so much algebra to those who have never felt it. But to those who have experienced the agony of wrestling, prevailing prayer, for the conversion of a soul, you may depend on it that the soul, after it is converted, appears as a dear child is to the mother. He has agonized for it, received it in answer to prayer and can present it before the Lord Jesus Christ saying, 'Behold, I and the children whom the Lord hath given me." (Isaiah 8:18)

"Another reason why God required this sort of prayer is that it is the only way in which the church can be properly prepared to receive great blessings without being injured by them. When the church is thus prostrated in the dust before God, and is in the depth of agonizing in prayer, the blessing does them good."

(P.72)

Story of John Knox – "John Knox was a man famous for his power in prayer, so that Queen

Mary of England used to say that she feared his prayers more than all the armies of Europe. Events showed that she had reason to do it. He used to be in such an agony for the deliverance of his country, that he could not sleep. He had a place in his garden where he used to go to pray. One night he and several friends were praying together, and as they prayed, Knox spoke and said that deliverance had come. He could not tell what had happened, but felt that something had taken place, for God had heard their prayers. What was it? Why? The next news they received was that, Mary was dead!

The following excerpts are from the autobiography of Charles Finney, by Fleming H. Revell. (pp.296, 297) Here Finney is talking about Abel Clary, a minister who gave himself wholly to prayer.

"He (Clary) had been licensed to preach, but his spirit of prayer was such, he was so burdened with the souls of men, that he was not able to preach much, his whole time and strength being given to prayer. The burden of his soul would frequently be so great that he was unable to stand, and he would writhe and groan in agony. "

Finney relates a story about a man who was renting a room to Mr. Clary.

"He is at my house and has been there for some time and I don't know what to think of him. I said, 'I have not seen him in any of our meetings.' 'No', he replied, 'he cannot go to meetings' he says, he prays nearly all the time, day and night and in such an agony of mind that I do not know what to make of it. Sometimes he cannot even stand on his knees, but will be prostrate on the floor and groan and pray in a manner that quite astonished me. I (Finney) said to the brother, I understand it; please keep still. It will come out all right, he will surely prevail. I knew of a considerable number of men who were exercised the same way in the same county; this Mr. Clary, and many others...partook of the same spirit and spent a good deal of their time in Rochester. This Mr. Clary continued in Rochester as long as I did and did not leave until after I had left. He never, that I could learn, appeared in public, but gave himself wholly to prayer."

This spirit of prayer, which was on many in Rochester during the second Great Awakening, I believe, was the main reason why the city of Rochester was swept through with revival like no other city in American history. To this day, the city of Rochester is the only American city that was ever taken for God (during the years 1830, 1831).

Read Finney's account of the revival in Rochester just a few pages later in his autobiography (p. 300):

> "The greatness of the work in Rochester, at that time, attracted so much of the attention of ministers and Christians throughout the State of New York, New England and in many parts of the United States. That the very fame of it was an efficient instrument in the hands of the spirit of God in promoting the greatest revival of religion throughout the land that this country had ever witnessed."

One person during this time living in Rochester said,

"I have been examining the records of the criminal courts and I find this striking fact that whereas our city has increased since that revival threefold, there is not one-third as many prosecutions for crime as there had been up until that time. Indeed, by the power of that revival, public sentiment has been molded. The public affairs of the city have been in a great measure in the hands of Christian men; and the controlling influences in the community have been on the side of Christ."

(Pp. 44, 45)

"The spirit of prayer was immediately poured out wonderfully upon the young converts. Before the week was out I learned that some of them, when they would attempt to observe this season of prayer, would lose all their strength and be unable to rise to their feet or even stand upon their knees in their closets; and that some would lay prostrate on the floor, and pray with unutterable groanings for the outpouring of the spirit of God."

(p. 148)

In another account, Finney talks about a man's wife who had a spirit of prayer on her to such an extent that her husband was very concerned.

> "Brother Finney, I think my wife will die. She is so exercised in her mind that she cannot rest day or night but is given up entirely to prayer. She has been all the morning, said he, in her room, groaning and struggling in prayer; and I am afraid it will entirely overcome her strength. Hearing my voice in the sitting room, she came out from her bedroom with a heavenly glow. She exclaimed, 'Brother Finney, the Lord has come!' This work will spread all over this region!'...I had witnessed such scenes before and believed that prayer had prevailed. The work went on, spread and prevailed..."

(p. 204)

> "In this revival, as in those that had proceeded, there was a very earnest spirit of prayer. We had a prayer meeting from house to house at 11:00a.m. At one of those meetings I recollect that a Mr. S_____, cashier of a bank in that city, was so pressed by the spirit of prayer, that when the meeting

was dismissed he was unable to rise from his knees, as we had all just been kneeling in prayer. He remained upon his knees, and writhed and groaned in agony. He said, pray for Mr. __, President of the bank of which he was cashier. This president was a wealthy, unconverted man. When it was seen that his soul was in travail for that man, the praying people knelt down and wrestled in prayer for his conversion. As soon as the mind of Mr. S_____ was relieved that he can go home, we all retired; and soon after, the president of the bank, for whom we prayed, expressed hope in Christ. He had not before this, I believe, attended any of the meetings; and it was not known that he was concerned about his salvation. But prayer prevailed, and God soon took his case in hand."

As anyone can see from all these accounts, the spirit of prayer, known in this book as "travail", was not uncommon to the church in the 1800's, but instrumental in promoting the revivals of the second Great Awakening in our country. I believe this spirit of travail is absolutely essential for this generation to see the next great harvest of souls come into the kingdom.

CHAPTER 8

TRAVAIL: TO REACH THE NATIONS

Isaiah 66:8 – "Who hath heard such a thing? Who hath seen such things? Shall the earth be made to bring forth in one day? Or shall a nation be born at once? For as soon as Zion travailed, she brought forth her children".

This verse is talking about giving birth to the earth, or to a nation. (Giving birth is a biblical term for salvation – see John 3:3-8.) The method it speaks of for this great move of salvation to encompass a whole nation or the world is "travail" (likening it to a woman travailing and giving birth to her children in the natural- in this passage it may or not be referring to travail as a form of prayer but the point is –travail is necessary to give birth to nations not only human babies).

Is there anywhere else in scripture where travail is alluded to in relation to bringing a nation or the earth to salvation? I believe there are and the following biblical principle will show us the importance of travail in God's mind to bringing the nations back to Himself.

The first verse we'll look at is Genesis 1:1, 2, "In the beginning God created the heaven and the earth. And the earth was without form, and void; and darkness was upon the face of the deep. And the Spirit of God moved upon the face of the waters."

Genesis 1:1 tells us that God created the universe. In Genesis 1:2, I believe we see in symbolic pictures why God created the universe. In this verse two words are used interchangeably that mean the same thing "deep" and "waters". The bible says that the spirit of God moved upon the face of the waters. Waters in this passage to me can also futuristically symbolize the multitudes of humanity (as it does in Isaiah 57:20; Revelation 20:13; Luke 5:4-6) although the original/primary meaning of waters in this particular passage is obviously not multitudes of people since humans didn't exist yet.

I believe this verse possibly illustrates in biblical symbolism that the purpose of God in creating the universe is that God's spirit desires face-to-face intimacy, with His people and the way to get there is to respond to the spirit's cry to the deepness of our soul.

> Psalm 42:7 – "Deep calleth unto deep at the noise of thy waterspouts; all thy waves and thy billows are gone over me".

This is another verse where deepness and water is connected to God's desire for intimacy with humanity, not just religious ritual. In reading Psalm 42 you'll see in the context a person's deep longing and thirsting for more of God and God reciprocating in the form of waves and waterspouts.

How does the spirit of God move multitudes of people? When His people respond to His spirit with a face-to-face encounter that comes out of the depth of their being.

Another biblical principle is found in John 7:37-39,

> "In the last day, that great day of the feast, Jesus stood and cried, saying, If any man thirst, let him come unto me, and drink. He that believeth on me, as the scripture hath said, out of his belly shall flow rivers of living water. But this spake he of the Spirit, which they that believe on him should receive: for the Holy Ghost was not yet given; because that Jesus was not yet glorified."

Hence, this is another instance where the Holy Spirit, water, and the inner most being of humanity is connected. Jesus was preaching this on the last and great day of the Feast of Tabernacles. Another name for this Feast is the "Feast of the Ingathering". (Exodus 23:16)

I believe the purpose of this feast was for the Jews to prophetically celebrate the ingathering of the Harvest; to call the nations back into covenant with God, which began to be fulfilled in the New

Testament. (Acts 15:16, 17; Matthew 28:19, 20 and Psalm 2:8, 9 -- The first fruits being on the day of Pentecost). During this seven-day feast, seventy bulls were sacrificed (Numbers 29:12-32). I believe one bull for every one of the original seventy nations found in Genesis Chapter 10.

Furthermore, at the end of this feast, the prophet Haggai prophesied that God would shake the heavens and the earth, the sea and the dry land and all the nations before His house would be filled with Glory.

> Haggai 2:1 – "In the seventh month, in the one and twentieth day of the month, came the word of the Lord by the prophet Haggai saying." (This is the last day of the Feast of the Ingathering).
>
> Haggai 2:6,7 – "For thus saith the Lord of hosts; Yet once, it is a little while, and I will shake the heavens, and the earth, and the sea, and the dry land; And I will shake all nations, and the desire of all nations shall come: and I

will fill this house with glory, saith the Lord of hosts." (Read also Zechariah 14:16)

Being intimately familiar with the Old Testament and how this feast points to His gathering the nations back to His Father, Jesus made some astonishing remarks. He talked about the belly, (signifying the deepness of a person's being) water and the Holy Spirit.

I believe He was correlating the feast of Tabernacles with how God was going to reach the nations—a move of God's Spirit out of the deepness of the believer's belly (or innermost being), i.e. a deep move of God within a believers being that would produce living water. Hold it you say! *I thought this verse was merely talking about an individual believers' receiving of the Holy Spirit at salvation?* It's talking about this as well but includes much more than this. (Remember, everything God does, including influencing a nation has to start with obedient and saved individuals). Because of what the Feast of

Tabernacles prophetically and scripturally implies, I believe Jesus was using the term living waters based on what Ezekiel prophesied about the coming Kingdom temple.

Let's look at Ezekiel 47:1-12.

> "Afterward he brought me again unto the door of the house; and, behold, waters issued out from under the threshold of the house eastward: for the forefront of the house stood toward the east, and the waters came down from under from the right house of the house, at the south side of the altar. Then brought he me out of the way of the gate northward, and led me about the way without unto the utter gate by the way that looketh eastward; and, behold, there ran out waters on the right side. And when the man that had the line in his hand went forth eastward, he measured a thousand cubits, and he brought me through the waters; the waters were to the ankles. Again he measured a thousand, and brought me through the waters; the waters were to the knees. Again he measured a thousand, and brought me through; the waters were to

the loins. Afterward he measured a thousand; and it was a river that I could not pass over: for the waters were risen, waters to swim in, a river that could not be passed over. And he said unto me, Son of man, hast thou seen this? Then he brought me, and caused me to return to the brink of the river. Now when I had returned, behold, at the bank of the river were very many trees on the one said and on the other. Then said he unto me, these waters issue out toward the east country, and go down into the desert, and go into the sea; which being brought forth into the sea, the waters shall be healed. And it shall come to pass, that everything that liveth, which moveth, withersoever the rivers shall come, shall live: and there shall be a very great multitude of fish, because these waters shall come thither: for they shall be healed; and everything shall live whither the river cometh. And it shall come to pass, that the fishers shall stand upon it from Engedi even unto Eneglaim; they shall be a place to spread forth nets; their fish shall be according to their kinds, as the fish of the great sea, exceeding many. But the miry places thereof and the marshes thereof shall not be healed; they shall be given to salt. And by the river upon the bank thereof, on this side and on that side, shall grow all trees for meat, whose leaf shall not fade, neither shall the fruit thereof be consumed: it shall bring forth new fruit according to his months, because their waters they issued out of the sanctuary: and the fruit thereof shall be meat, and the leaf thereof for medicine."

These passages of scripture are talking about living waters (at first starting out with individuals like a trickle, than water only up to the ankles, then getting greater and greater as more and more people participate in this flood of Glory) proceeding from the temple or tabernacle of God that go forth and bring in a multitude of fish and bring healing to the world.

In conclusion, Jesus stood up on that last and great day of the feast of Tabernacles because it was He as the Word who became flesh and "tabernacled" among us (literal Greek rendering of John 1:14).

Consequently it is only by looking to Him and seeking God out of the depths of our belly that enables the Father to send living waters that give birth to His purpose to heal the nations. The feast of Tabernacles will ultimately be fulfilled when Jesus hands all the nations back to the Father and God makes the whole earth His tabernacle. (Read 1 Corinthians 15:24 and Revelation 21:3)

Isaiah 66:8 talks about Zion (which can also symbolize the church)[3] travailing and giving birth to children who will take the nations and the earth to the Lord!

Ezekiel prophesied that life-giving waters would come out of the temple of God (1 Corinthians 6:19 says Christians are God's temple). Jesus prophesied that living waters of the Spirit would come out of our bellies (where a pregnant woman holds her baby until she goes into travail and gives birth) which will give new life to multitudes of fish

---

[3] Hebrews 12:22,23

(people) that will result in healing the land (Isaiah 66:8 calls it bringing forth the earth).

To me it is clear that God's only remedy for a sick and lost humanity is that believers (as God's bride) so passionately and deeply desire His face on the earth that they enable God's Spirit to intermingle deeply with their human spirits which results in a travail (pregnancy) that gives birth to His will and the destiny of the Nations.

It may not be an easy, "quick fix", "blab it grab it" solution, but it is God's will that we enter into fellowship with the sufferings of Christ before we attain unto the resurrection of the dead (giving birth to dead people and reviving purposes that were once dead because of sin; Read Philippians 3:10, 11).

In the Bible the cross came before the resurrection, Calvary before Pentecost, death before life, judgment before mercy, (in the Levitical sacrificial system) and mourning before comfort. (Matthew 5:4)

So many only want the blessings of God or the power of God. The baptism of the Spirit without the baptism of fire or the Kingdom without the cup (Mark 10:37, 38). God wants us to embrace the cross now and to travail in agony of soul now so we can share in His glory later on.

CHAPTER 9

CONCLUSION

You may be wondering whatever happened in my city (NYC) as a result of the prayer meeting mentioned in Chapter 1. Well, the truth of the matter is that it was only the first of many such intense times of corporate prayer for our city in the following six months, some with only our local church, some citywide "consecration assemblies".

In the last consecration assemblies during that time there was a great release in the spirit for our city after a protracted time of repentance, spiritual warfare and intense travail. While we didn't receive any specific prophetic words assuring us of the result, there seemed to be a sense that much of God's pending judgment against our city was modified somewhat (though we can't say for sure, there was also a sense that a strong move of God was coming as well).

Consequently there was more and more unity in the body of Christ in our city which prepared us for the terrorist attacks of September 11th 2001. For several years myself and other intercessors in our church and city had a sense that imminent danger was at our door, hence our intense prayer. Although our prayer did not stop the attacks I believe that without the intense prayer, the terrorists would have been even more successful in their devious plans.

I hope and pray that this book doesn't only give information but carries with it an impartation to pray as never before. I believe that God wants us to begin to identify with His pain, bear His burdens and enter into His sufferings. Like Jesus, we will see the result of the travail of our soul be satisfied (Isaiah 53:11) and witness the greatest revival we have ever seen.

However, we the Church need to mature. We need to go past merely praying through laundry lists of prayer requests, go beyond perfunctory prayers in corporate gatherings and go beyond just looking for renewal-type experiences.

God may use some experiences to renew us, but after we are restored let us move on to perfection (*maturity* – Hebrews 6:1). God is looking for a people that can share His burdens and then give His solutions; heaven-born solutions that will transform whole communities. One person in travail cannot do this. There is a remnant of people in every congregation, in every community, that God is just waiting to fill with a mighty spirit of prayer that can prevail with Him and send the enemy fleeing.

We have had many strategies come to light in recent years that have greatly blessed the Body of Christ. We have had thousands of conferences on revival and much understanding in the way of spiritual warfare, personal deliverance, unity, racial reconciliation, spiritual mapping, the prophetic, apostolic leadership and on the Kingdom of God. All this illumination and we still haven't seen one city in the U.S. fall under the glory of God.

Unfortunately, it's one thing to go to a conference to learn strategies and try to put them into practice. It's another thing to see multitudes of people in every region of the U.S. marked with a mighty spirit of prayer and giving birth to the strategies God wants to use right now (read Ezekiel 9:4).

If we are not careful, we will merely have a bunch of people running around reading books and knowing the history of revivals instead of opening themselves up to God's heart and letting the Spirit of God supernaturally pray out His burdens in us. I believe in informed intercession, however, I also know that in the bible it teaches us what God does when we don't know how (or what) to pray for as we should (uninformed intercession).

Historical research and spiritual mapping are good but not enough. Believers need to allow the

Spirit to pray through them with groans that words cannot utter. (Romans 8:26) This is what multitudes did in the past and this is what happened in Rochester before that city was taken in the early 19th century.

If we are not careful, the Church will be attempting to do with mere information what can only be done with Holy Spirit impartation and impregnation through travail.

If we are not careful, we will have multitudes of Christians randomly attacking the "high places of a city" (because it worked in another region) even though God has shown us that influence over a land is only released when the people of God are properly prepared and positioned to steward it, and care for it (Deuteronomy 7:22). What properly positions and prepares the Church initially for influence more than prayer, intercession and travail.

We also need to have a plan to enact generational influence through our biological families. Read my book "Walk in Generational Blessing" for more on this topic.

Without the Spirit and burden of God praying through us, even God-given strategies and methods can become gimmicks, quick-fixes and fleshly exercises that will only give the saints another excuse not to yield themselves totally to God, seeking His face and allowing the Spirit to pray through us for His purposes.

Let's believe God together for millions of Christians to be totally given over to God in travail, to give birth to the greatest revival the world has ever known. A move of God that doesn't only cause church growth and renewal, but one that shakes whole kingdoms, redeems cultures, and brings about flourishing cities.

About the author:

Joseph Mattera is in demand internationally as a speaker and consultant. His mission is to influence leaders who influence nations. To order one of his four books or to subscribe to his weekly newsletter go to www.josephmattera.org

http://www.josephmattera.org

Joseph Mattera's list of other published books are Ruling in the Gates, Kingdom Revolution, Kingdom Awakening and Walk in Generational Blessings.

Made in the
USA
Monee, IL